A Season and a Time

Also by Maurice Whelan and published by Ginninderra Press

Boat People
The Lilac Bow
Excalibur's Return

Maurice Whelan

A Season and a Time

Acknowledgements

I am grateful to many people who read my poems.
I am particularly indebted to the following:
Lena Bruselid, Gary Bryson, Michael Dudley, Tony Earls,
Judy Griffiths, Winton Higgins, Richard O'Neill-Dean,
Lorraine Rose, Anthony Whelan, Gemma Whelan, Louise Whelan,
Bob White.
Their comments and criticisms have improved my writing;
its failings are my own.

My poem 'Engrafting New' uses lines from three Seamus Heaney poems ('Mossbawn-Sunlight', 'Postscript' and 'Clearances 8') and also uses words from his essay 'The Government of the Tongue'.

My thanks to Lucy East and Jordan East for the front page image.

My continuing thanks to Stephen Matthews for publishing my work.

A Season and a Time
ISBN 978 1 74027 843 0
Copyright © text Maurice Whelan 2014

First published 2014
Reprinted 2015

GINNINDERRA PRESS
PO Box 3461 Port Adelaide SA 5015
www.ginninderrapress.com.au

Contents

A Season and a Time	7
Downside Up	15
A Poem	16
Echo	17
Togetherness	18
A Passion	19
You Had To Be There	21
The Sacred Silent and Sublime	22
Gungarlin Heights	27
From 24,000 Feet to 6 Down Under	29
Dead Rosella	31
The Call	32
Introibo ad Altare Dei	33
The Mandolin	34
We Don't Talk These Days	37
Engrafting New	39
My Place on Earth	41

To T.P.

A Season and a Time

'To everything there is a season and a time
for every purpose under the heavens.' – Ecclesiastes 3:1

A time to be born and a time to die

>When I place a seashell on your hand
>>stand at your side and gaze at a yellow sunset
>>the moon paints our faces silver-white,
>
>When I tell you to close your eyes
>>listen to a Heaney poem
>>a song by Joni Mitchell or Leonard Cohen,
>
>When I take your hand and we walk in the bush
>>inhale moist air overladen
>>with sweet eucalyptus,
>
>>I see a moment of your birth my child.
>>I meet a moment of my death my child.

A time to plant

and trust seeds
sown in the soil
of a fertile mind.

A time to harvest

> the shoals of memories,
> the moments of our past,
> that swim the oceans of our lives.
> While we are wanderers
> we mingle with the currents.
> When safe upon the shore
> we cast the nets.

A time to kill

vain promise and pursuit
abandon barren ground
from which no new leaf or stem or flower or fruit
will ever spring.

A time to heal

> like a tree
> which when attacked
> receives the blow
> weeps sorrow
> permits the gnarled lump
> – which some call unsightly –
> to harden and protect.

A time to weep

tears
like raindrops that gather
on jacaranda leaves
released
to fall
to nourish thirsty ground.

A time to laugh

to cackle, to chortle, to chuckle, to giggle,
to guffaw, to hoot, to snigger, to snort, to titter,

because
there's nothing like it on earth.
Laughter
what god-almighty genius invented it?

A time to mourn

throw open the doors,
welcome the visiting guests
sorrow sadness lamentation.
Accept the storm of grief
as it rages
racks the body to its foundations.
Grief – the price you pay for love.

A time to dance

    the courtship dance of mourning doves,
    the water dance of the Great Crested Grebe.
    Leap like a gazelle.
    Vault the world.

A time to lose

what once was good but is now a husk
a wraith
a pale reflection of its former glory.

A time to seek

    new paths
    where fresh green buds are on the trees
    and spring flowers weep beauty.

A time to keep

time precious.
Watch the changing colour of each moment
hear the pause between the notes
the music inside the words.

A time to cast away

and be a castaway.
Play with the world
this round-flat thing
this exasperating enthralling absurdity.
Require all leaders to explain themselves.
Do not become old
before you become wise.

A time to embrace

a friend who will be a mainstay
of your life
present when far away
one who has the gift of tongues
and is blessed with the gift of silence.

A time to refrain from embracing

those who are best enjoyed
at a safe distance
seen now and then
allowed to touch
selected parts of a life
the rest kept separate and safe.

A time to rend

split an orchid's packed root system
with an axe, strenuously.
Half measures will not bear fruit.

    A time to sew

    the damaged flesh of youth.
    Wear scars not as a blemish
    but as a mark of learning.

A time to cast away stones

flat round ones to be sent in a reverse spin
skimming the glass surface of a lake.
A dozen hops deserve a hurrah.

    A time to gather stones

    from all corners of our life
    from the beaches mountains
    and riverbeds of our world
    jewels of the earth glowing glistening gliding
    through the mountains and the seas
    and the river beds of our remembrance.

A time to keep silence

sacred.
Let its luscious light
brighten dull corners
in restless minds.

A time to speak

out.
Overcome the fear of being the only one
the single voice that takes a stand
that says no.
Speak quietly
hold your head high.
Shout at the top of your voice
if that's what it takes.
And if you have to listen to tales
told by an idiot signifying nothing
find a new storyteller.

A time to love

to give love.
To receive love –
it's harder than you think.

A time to hate

and be a good hater
of humbug
of all that's wasteful and absurd.

A time for war

when the fragile ramparts
erected to protect
the innocents
are breached.

A time for peace

that is worn proudly
like a garment woven
from necessity
from the threads of our infirmities
to clothe our nakedness
to safeguard our restless sleep.

Downside Up

In the still water
a white-winged eel shimmers
shows its belly
trails its thin smoky tail.

In the air above
a jet plane chalks the sky
appears out of one river bank
disappears inside another.

A Poem

It all came late that year
spring was its usual beginning
but the shoots delayed and
showed no sign of breaking ground.

At first light on the first day of the new year
it sprung
from nowhere
its verdant virginal vocabularies

holding hands and dancing.
It was light in its step
free in its freedom
wild in its wildness.

It declared to me it only needed solitude
and that elusive pitch of perfect stillness
and added, when longing dies
and dictionaries disassemble

new words spring forth from the songs of birds.
And thinking my lesson over
I made to move away only
to be pulled back and sat and told

all speech began listening to birds
in the beginning was the song
and the song became flesh
and dwelt among us.

Echo

Below the tree-top screeching
of the sulphur-crested cockatoo
are smaller sounds

Rosella drinks morning dew
Magpie warbles
the flap of wagtail wings
louder than its call recalls

the sudden heavy flap of pheasant flight
the darting fluttering path of snipe
a murder of ravens that leaves nothing in its wake
the distant crek-crek call of the lonely corncrake.

Togetherness

Earth was first and will be last.
Flowers bloomed before us and will hereafter;
yet the tree knows not its treeness,
its present or its past; not the rose its beauty.

The sun in all its glory knows
not the pinkness of its rising and
paints red and yellow settings
for others' eyes to see.

Water mirrors us but not itself.
The mind sees the mind that sees.
A face reflects another and every day
new wordless galaxies are born.

Only lovers of this world
see its beauty, but one day we
will depart and leave Earth alone.
Never to be known again; never again loved.

A Passion

To T.P.

I met a man today.
I'd met that man before,
before his body reneged on its promise
to be the vessel of vitality,
only now and again to complain
of ache and pain and passing illness.

His mind still brightly shines
his heart beats strong and warm.
A passer-by would say
there's a sparkle in that man's eye.

Were I he and my vessel
refused my bidding
I would become
a god.

As Poseidon the Earth-Shaker my wrath would be
ungovernable.
I'd scorch the mountain tops,
scald the valleys.
My rage would smash the rock face,
foul the skies with plumes of toxic ash and purple darkness.
I'd curse Fate and the injustice of it all.

I would wield my power to make myself a king.
I…I…

Alas like Lear I'd be a king without a kingdom.
A most poor weak man made tame to fortune's blows.
A man crying

I am bound
Upon a wheel of fire, that mine own tears
Do scald like molten lead.

I'd hope, when my waves of grief and fury did subside,
to have a light in my mind to shine,
a heart that beats strong and warm,
a wry smile when the passer-by says
there's a sparkle in that man's eye.

You Had To Be There

On seeing Michael Dauth play *The Lark Ascending*

You had to be there
no two ways about it
because when all is said and heard
only the eyes can see.

It was the way he stood.
He played his last note –
the violin rested under his chin
the conductor's hands lowered

the orchestra and choir rested –
but his bow moved on and up in the air
his arm outstretched and there it remained
as if poised to play unseen strings.

The whole opera house was still
yes if a pin had dropped we'd all have
heard it…it was as if the bow had a life
all its own as if an invisible thread

of music joined the now invisible lark
and the lark had lost itself inside an exaltation
of larks soaring inside the hazy blueness of the
sky with the thrilling quivering songs and strings

ascending with the soaring birds
singing on playing on in the heavens.
Before fulsome applause there was hesitation.
Our spellbound eyes framed that silent moment.

I'm right, aren't I? You had to be there.

The Sacred Silent and Sublime

Choirmaster

Look how his body leans
his lips shape their song
his hands guide the liquid music
through the coral cathedral

of the Great Barrier Reef uncloistered
creatures clownfish parrotfish
sea anemones angelfish trumpet fish
in cacophonies of colour crimson emerald

purple powder-blue sapphire
red yellow green orange
swim and sway and drift in perfect
harmony alto soprano tenor bass.

Can you hear song beams descending
from the vault of heaven piercing
the heart can you see the chancel flooding
with blue-green dancing dusty sparkling sea?

A Calling

The call went out.
He stood still for a long time
and set off in an easterly direction.

The caller had said –
'If you are found worthy
your hands will be anointed
to you it will be given
to be the reader of the sacred texts'.

The springtime of his departure became winterish
the landscape through which he walked
flowerless treeless grassless.
The promise did not come to pass
and he returned dispirited and depleted.

Listening deep into many a long night
into the workings of his own mind
with much practice and patience
and learning over many years
he found his own voice.

Then he found silence.

And having no need to speak for himself
he became the mouthpiece
of wind and rain and storm and sea
of forest and flower and scrub and weed

of mountain and sky and river and stream
of snow and ice and bog and swamp
of desert and lake and rock and sand
of the voiceless ocean
of the mute land
of this sacred earth.

Over Beyond

With the dawn of each new day
we can as the poet Bashō advised
become a tree a flower a stone a stream
a ray of sunlight
place ourselves inside another world
borrow senses not our own
the senses that are beyond us.

Time travel will present no obstacles
fifteen billion years can be traversed
in one imaginative leap
to make the journey
from the beginning
to the end of time we simply
catapult ourselves into the unknown
the places that are beyond us.

And if our minds and hearts
are up to it
we can walk that coast
that dividing line that marks the edge
of the expanding universe
from the void?
the emptiness?
the nothingness?
the mysteries that are beyond us.

In evening time it is the time
to let it all go
leave Andromeda to the Andromedeans
cease gallivanting through the galaxies
traipsing across Orion
skating round the rings of Saturn
become ourselves again
hear the beating heart
pa-pum pa-pum pa-pum pa-pum
the almost-silent breath
savour the signs of precious life
the gift that is beyond us.

Are We There Yet

He owned his own church. It was small –
like St Kevin's at Glendalough in County Wicklow
Ireland or the Church of San Carlos Borroméo
at Carmel in Monterey County California –

and it was very beautiful. It wasn't real, of course.
No. It was complete in his mind,
so he could take it with him
all the time, wherever he went.

He would slip away when he was with you,
you never noticed because
when you talked and he listened
he gave his full attention.

And only later, after he'd gone
did you know he had quietly
taken you there, and the two of you
had stood together in silent prayer.

Gungarlin Heights

For John, Meera and Nick

In the high country you are close to heaven.

The Gungarlin was lake-blue; it was river-brown
depending on the angle of the sun,
on which side of the metal bridge you looked down from.

A gang-gang cockatoo family perched among reeds at the river's edge,
their calls like creaky gates, their crested red heads
and mild-grey plumage mirrored on the smooth surface of the water.

When darkness came the temperature dropped below freezing.
Sleep was hard to come by and the night was long.
Stumbling from the brittle, frosted tents our sufferings were soon forgot.
A silver celestial veil draped the hills, rocks, trees, grass and ground,
as if all the stars of the firmament had come among us – as if
we were chosen witnesses to a visitation from above.
Space was at a premium and every part of every object near and far
flickered and sparkled and silvered in the brisk morning light.

Built the fire; boiled the billy.
A stockman and a wedged-tailed eagle came and went.
Neither acknowledged our presence.
The eagle soared gracefully, tilted and effortlessly swung away.
The stockman was comfortable in the saddle.

The stockman's mare climbed the brown grassy hill
turning this way, that way, making it easy for herself.
Beneath the surface of the cool meandering river
the trout were doing the same thing, moving
this way, that way. They were busy feeding on nymphs.
That's what we said to ourselves, and to each other.
The trout didn't acknowledge our presence either.

So, apart from the serious business of catching fish,
other business presented and required our attentions.
I suppose that's the way it's meant to be.
That's the way it was.
We got what we came for,
even though we left empty-handed.

In the high country you are close to heaven and to earth.

From 24,000 Feet to 6 Down Under

Ningaloo, Western Australia, May 2013

The flight from Perth to Learmonth had
few culinary pleasures many visual delights.

Flat brown land fields squared
angled with a giant geometry set,
                precision measured.

Mile wide mine roads uncoiled,
springs straightened, stretched,
                signposted infinity.

Dry creek beds on red-brown ochre earth,
silhouettes of fallen trees,
                veins and arteries.

From up above the beaches' band of foam is still,
foam and sand, cream and white
                twinned ribbons.

Lower down, cloud clusters, unmade stacks,
white hay on a vast invisible field of glass
                awaited gathering.

On the road to Coral Bay brown cone-shaped termite
mounds recalled a greener land, an emerald isle,

1950s Ireland where sweet green meadows
felled became cone-like stacks of golden hay.

Snorkelling at Turquoise Bay, six feet under,
a school of bright blue tiny fish
                patrolled the coral.

Beyond the reef a whale shark the largest fish in the sea
– they grow to eighteen metres long –
        caught my eye,

displayed no interest in patrolling me.
His metre-wide mouth sifted krill and plankton,
        a gigantic body,

dot painted by an underwater dreamtime dot painter,
glided with ease my tentative art
        ocean swimming,

no match for his grace and gentle beauty,
his ease in what is his own earth, his watery version
        of terra firma.

This once was our ancestral home,
this liquid land, this garden of delight,
        a magic universe.

Dead Rosella

On the roadside
motionless
tiny talons
curl and cling
to invisible wire.

This beautiful bird belongs
to flight
to air
to darting tree lines
to another.

Lost to its world
its skies
its wings
like fallen angels' wings
frozen in final flight.

The Call

Hello. Thanks for ringing.
I'm well yes I'm well.
Good to hear your voice.
And you?
I was thinking of you the moment the phone rang.
A coincidence! No. No. I don't think so.
Because I think of you a lot.
Because these days you are often in my mind.

Introibo ad Altare Dei

'I will go unto the altar of God' – Psalm 42

Would to God
God's imposters'

Raven-black
Blighted shadows

Spared the leaf
The stem the shoot

The fragrant
Flower of youth.

The Mandolin

Its first life began in Naples
1919 in a craftsman's workshop
a teardrop-shaped bowl an echo chamber
fashioned from wood.
Who knows how many hands held
and played those strings
how many ears heard its tunes
how many times O Solo Mio
and other airs were sung
what loving what sorrowing
encircled its delicate frame.

My father went to Italy
had an audience with Pope Paul VI
returned with the Papal blessing and the mandolin.
Large farmer's hands worked the frets
fingers and thumb plucked the double strings
or with tremulous pick called forth The Coolin
Danny Boy and The Cuckoo Waltz.

In time in age in death
the mandolin passed to me and I
with more love than talent
failed to make it sing
and then in my new home in my new land
in the Australian heat the mandolin cracked
and became forever dumb.

You'd think that would be the end of the story
the end of the mandolin but enter
from the land of the rising sun
Edward Shimada an alchemist.

Three months ago the mandolin went to his workshop.
Tonight transformed it returned to my home in Sydney
a new being a bird in flight the teardrop-shaped bowl its body
the neck intact and the transplanted inner parts of an old piano
are now my bird's legs and tail and head and wings.

Tonight my home is a museum
and the spirits of all who heard
and played the mandolin are filing past
eyes widen fingers silence startled lips
a hush goes down the line
beings from a still world
know full well how perfect
is the music that rests in silence.

Their long procession thins
a late straggler enters my father's shade
with hands joined at the small of his back
he wryly smiles surveys the scene
I speak I say that while my talent failed
my love for him and for the mandolin
outstripped all expectation.

There's a rush of words from within.
'I saw you yesterday an old photo
1929 you were twelve sitting cross-legged on grass
your face on fire with fun
there was eagerness in your body
when the camera released you
you'd have sprung to your feet
risen and taken the high ball
sent it sailing over the bar.

'Your mellow tenor tones
your sinewy textured songs
your heartfelt playing
echoed that triumphant youth.
Lay down the dumb mandolin.
Speak to me now.'

Music always was for him a stronger suit
than words so as my yearning grows
his shade weakens departs and I stand
my hands at the small of my back.

It's time to count my blessings.
I give thanks for my bird-mandolin
its earth-bound journey is complete
its heaven-bound flight begun.

We Don't Talk These Days

We don't talk these days
the way we used to
and when we do
it seems one-sided
I supply the words
she the listening.

The other day there was something
I wanted to tell her.
It had to do with plates dinner plates
blue patterned dinner plates with a country scene

in Japan or is it China
a scene of mountains trees and gardens
tea gardens and a small human figure
stands beside a bridge or gate or lake
a figure so small you could
if you're not careful not see it at all.

Someone told me you shouldn't
look upon the scene from where you stand
it is better to observe from the little figure's
point of view
there's a new angle
other things different things to see
there's more to find if you look that way
I was told.

I wanted to tell her that.

I imagined when I spoke
the widening eyes
lips parted in awe
a child-like smile of wonder
at knowledge that was new.

But, you know, she did that all her life
became the little figure
found a new angle
saw things inside me
I didn't know were there.

It is a strange fact but true
the dead can be more present
do more seeing more listening
than the ones we call the living.

Engrafting New

So far I've avoided the obituaries,
The great eulogies. Later perhaps.
For now, mourning is quiet; house private.
I have him all to myself.

His passing was a great blow.
Sure we were just getting used to
McGahern going when this fellow
Heaney ups and leaves for good.

Is there anyone else to turn to?
Hold on! It is as he'd foretold it'd be:
Big soft buffetings come at the car sideways
Catch the heart off guard…blow it open.

A spring dawn enters the room.
His poems enter my heart,
Crisp as a silvered frost,
Fresh as a first reading.

And when I speak them loudly,
His deep-planted words flow leisurely.
There's a new step in my voice.
I'm hearing things I've never heard.

The light that is his shadow shines,
Shows new paths, ceises, crossings,
Stepping stones, stairways to
Richer, deeper, greener, inner lands.

The space he has vacated is for us,
Luminous emptiness.
A warp and waver of light.
Sunlit absence.

The heft and hush of him is now
A bright nowhere,
A soul ramifying and forever
Silent, beyond silence listened for.

My Place on Earth

A solid monument a stone wall ten feet high fifty feet long
stands as witness and there is no breath no sign of life
there is peace all is quiet the quiet and the peace that lives
where life has passed and yes the silence stretches into infinity.

A visitor today a newcomer to this place might remark
upon the unremarkable stone wall ten feet high fifty feet long.
It's a boundary wall between a garden and a haggard.

I've been here before fifty years ago this wall was
the back wall of a long line of sheds that housed cattle.

Stand with me where that row of daffodils bloom
along this line another wall stood with wooden rafters shouldering
a red corrugated iron V-shaped roof that covered three sheds
one for milking cows one for bullocks one for calves.

Come and step over the daffodils past the crocuses
and the budding roses step into the middle shed
into the middle of an Irish winter
walk between the bullocks their steamy breath like mist
rising from a marsh these big brutes spend their time
eating farting shitting butting they'll brush up
against you but no harm will come of that.

It's the middle of summer now and the shed's been empty for weeks
the beasts spend the milder months outdoors
we used to fill a sack full of straw and tie a rope to the rafters
a perfect swing and here in the manger
in that small clump of uneaten hay the Rhode Island Red
would lay her eggs and old Danny Gearon
with waistcoat and blue-striped collarless shirt
stood at the farmhouse door the eggs in his hat
and our mother scolded us and told us
to stop sniggering and staring at Danny's
pasty-white bald-headed eagle head.

Next door where the cows were milked
was a quieter place a loose chain around the beasts' necks
kept them separate and safe
here time passed unnoticed and when I sat on the wooden stool
pail between my knees my head resting against her hip
ready to push if I felt the kick
the sharp rat-a-tat-tat of the milk as it hit the metal base
turned to a soft rhythmic purr as the pail filled
creamy whiteness rising swaying holding my world in balance.

In the top shed many a calf came into the world and hit the
strawed floor with a thud its mother's tongue licking it to
life urging it on and up uncertain legs unwavering
instinct finding the mother's teat drawing the beestings.

Come around to the haggard – or rickyard as it was sometimes called –
the life that went on here was anyone's business
as a boy – I was three or four – I remember the old thrashing mill
the sheaves pitched up and fed down into its belly
dust flew hessian bags filled with golden grain
loose straw spewed out the back
and the chaffman with stinging eyes and golden beard
a latter-day Hermes demoted in the ranks
caduceus turned pitchfork in hand.

That was July or August but June now June was a much-loved month
the swaying meadows row upon verdant row bowed to the
sun-god whose love and light performed a trans-substantiation
from green to gold-nectared crackle-dry sweet-smelling hay
domes of architectural delight dotted the fields
and the hay bogey like a magic carpet with ropes and rackets
conspired like faith to move mountain after small mountain
and deliver them into the expert sculptural hands of the rickman.

Inside the wide-eyed trusting stillness of childhood
we neither travel back nor venture forth
time is unmeasured because it can't be measured
life is lived in the fragrance of the present
each single silent-movie scene
       – dust motes in a shaft of sunlight
       – a belching monster mill
       – a god of chaff in amber preserved
       – a bullock's watchful eye
       – soft yellow hoofs on a new-born calf
       – three brown eggs in a well-worn hat
       – pail brim-full of warm milk
       – the sweet sweet smell of new-mown hay
cradles and caresses you in its angel wings
moment by moment by sacred moment.

I can see that life has increased and other lives have flourished
and multiplied since I've been here
and if truth be told this piece of earth and this place
in its present form and manifestations and me
are strangers now people walk this earth
drive tractors and combine harvesters
dig gardens plant daffodils and crocuses and roses
that never knew me to forget me
and the ground where once my
world stood and was all I knew
is to them unknown unknowable and never to be mourned.

www.ingramcontent.com/pod-product-compliance
Lightning Source LLC
Chambersburg PA
CBHW062206100526
44589CB00014B/1978